Slavery in the United States

Slavery in the United States

Shirlee P. Newman

Watts LIBRARY

Franklin Watts
A Division of Grolier Publishing
New York • London • Hong Kong • Sydney
Danbury, Connecticut

For children everywhere, especially Haley

Note to readers: Definitions for words in **bold** can be found in the Glossary at the back of this book.

Photographs ©: Art Resource, NY: 32, 36, 40 (National Portrait Gallery, Smithsonian Institution, Washington D.C.); Brown Brothers: 51; Corbis-Bettmann: 5 bottom, 24 (Francis G. Mayer), 5 top, 27, 29; Jay Mallin: 44; Mary Evans Picture Library: 9 (Illustrated London News, 14 April, 1849, page 237), 37; Massachusetts Historical Society: 22; New Haven Colony Historical Society: 11; North Wind Picture Archives: 2, 12, 13, 14, 15, 17, 18, 20, 31, 34, 35, 39, 47, 50; Stock Montage, Inc.: 28 (The Newberry Library), 6, 10, 42, 43; Superstock, Inc.: 49.

Visit Franklin Watts on the Internet at:
http://publishing.grolier.com

Library of Congress Cataloging-in-Publication Data

Newman, Shirlee Petkin.
    Slavery in the United States / by Shirlee P. Newman
        p.   cm.— (Watts Library)
    Includes bibliographical references and index.
    ISBN 0-531-11695-6 (lib. bdg.)   0-531-16541-8 (pbk.)
    1. Slavery—United States—History—Juvenile literature. 2. Slaves—United States—Social conditions—Juvenile literature. [1. Slavery.] I. Title. II. Series.
E441 .N58   2000
973'.0496—dc21   00-038194

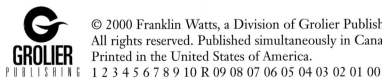

Contents

The first slaves arrived in the English colonies from Africa in the early 1600s.

Chapter One

The Slave Trade

Slavery in the United States began with a few boatloads of Africans who arrived in the thirteen colonies during the 1600s. However, the slave trade did not become a thriving business until the mid-1700s. By then, large **plantations** in the South had been developed, and their owners wanted slaves to work in their fields and homes. Slaves entered the colonies through several ports, but Charleston, South Carolina, was the busiest slave port of all.

A Slaver Who Gave Up the Trade

After making his fortune as a slave trader (or slaver) in Charleston, Henry Laurens, who was also a plantation owner, stopped trading for slaves. Most of his profits came from slaves captured by English friends. When the Revolutionary War ended, he helped the colonists reach a peace agreement with Britain.

The slave trade had been a profitable business in Europe long before it started in the colonies. European explorers who sailed down Africa's West Coast in the early 1400s reported that they had seen well-planned cities and powerful states with rich traditions of art, music, and religion. Later, however, when European slave traders went to Africa, they said that the people there were uncivilized, lived terrible lives, and would be better off in Europe or its colonies. Europeans from all walks of life made money through slave trading. Kings and queens, bankers, doctors, shipbuilders, sea captains, shopkeepers, mill owners, and anyone else who invested money in slaving expeditions, shared the profits.

European slave traders persuaded African leaders to wage war against one another and take prisoners. Then the leaders would have more slaves to trade with the Europeans for goods, such as cooking utensils, fabrics, beads, guns, gunpowder, liquor, and food-stuffs. The slave traders also hired Africans to raid the villages, kidnap children and adults, and march them in chains to the coast where ships waited to take them across the sea.

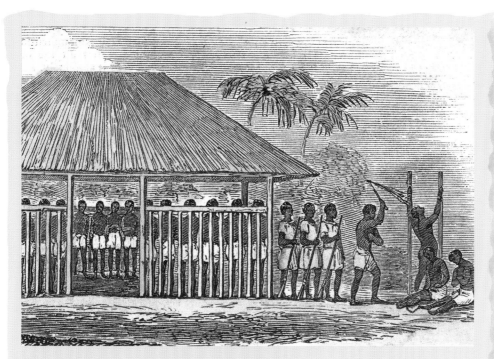

Storage Places for Slaves in Africa

While they waited for ships, some slaves were kept in outdoor pens, or jails called **barracoons**. Other slaves were chained together and kept in damp, dark dungeons under castles or forts built by Europeans, or in gloomy basements under slave traders' homes.

Slave traders tightly packed the slaves into lower decks of their ships. Many of the slaves died during the journey because of dreadful overcrowding, filth, spoiled food, and unclean water. Some slaves jumped overboard and drowned before they could be taken to the lower decks. When slaves tried to starve themselves to death, sailors inserted a metal instrument into their mouths. The instrument kept their mouths open while food was poured down their throats.

Revolts at Sea

Some Africans rebelled against being enslaved. A Spanish ship called the *Amistad* is a well-known revolt at sea. The slave trade had been illegal in the United States since 1808, but Africans were still being kidnapped and sold into slavery in 1839. That year, some African slaves took over the *Amistad* off the coast of Cuba. The Africans killed the ship's captain, and ordered a Spaniard on board to steer the ship back to Africa. He said he would, but he sailed north instead. American sailors boarded the ship in New York and put the Africans in prison.

Some of the slaves on the Amistad *fought the ship's crew and took over the ship.*

Kale, an eleven-year-old boy, learned to read and write English while the *Amistad* Africans were in prison. He wrote a letter to John Quincy Adams, a lawyer, former president, and congressman. Adams defended the Africans before the Supreme Court. The Court decided to free the slaves from the *Amistad* in 1841. After his release from jail, Joseph Cinque, the leader of the revolt, returned to Africa. Returning home, he learned that his family had been sold into slavery.

Many of the slave ships came to the port of Charleston, South Carolina.

Chapter Two

Life as a Slave

After the difficult sea voyage to the United States, slaves faced life in an unfamiliar land. "More than a third of us died on the passage," Charles Ball wrote. "It was more than a week after I left the ship before I could straighten my limbs." Slaves who arrived in Charleston, South Carolina, spent their first ten days in the **pest house**—a holding place for sick people—on an island in the harbor. Then slave traders took the healthy slaves ashore and auctioned them off.

An auctioneer sells a slave mother and child.

Injured or sick slaves were left in the pest house to die or sold them at discount prices. Most of the slaves never saw their families or friends again.

Many traders sold their slaves through auctions. Harriet Jacobs, an escaped slave, wrote about a woman who had been auctioned off along with her seven children. A man in the same town bought the woman. A slave trader from another town bought her children, and refused to tell her where he was taking them. "Gone!" the woman cried as her children were led away. "All gone! Why doesn't God kill me?"

Life In The South

Some southern plantations were small, and had only a few slaves. Other plantations were huge and had hundreds of slaves. On large plantations, the owner and his family lived in what was called the "Big House." House slaves cleaned, cooked, served meals, and took care of children. Some house slaves slept in attics or closets or corners in the Big House, even though their families lived in the slave quarters. Slaves also worked in small buildings on the plantation. They wove cloth in the weaving house and dyed cloth in the dye house. They made tools and horseshoes in the blacksmith shop, and furniture and coffins in the carpentry shop.

Even the slave children worked. They began carrying food and water when they were about six years old. By the age of twelve, they did the same jobs as adults. ". . . As soon as they [children] are able to work out[side] I expect to reap

Many southern slaves lived in small cabins, such as the ones shown below.

the benefit of their labor," George Washington wrote to his overseers.

Slaves who worked in the fields lived in tiny cabins, usually at the back of the property. Solomon Northrup, a field slave, wrote that when he worked on a cotton plantation the driver, or overseer, followed the slaves on horseback with a whip, and that whip was flying from morning till night. Northrup also worked on a sugar plantation. He said that slaves on sugar plantations cut cane for hours under the blistering sun and stirred hot, steaming cane juice in big open pots.

Josiah Henson, another field slave, wrote: "Our clothes were made of the coarsest cloth, and we were given one pair of shoes a year. We lived in one-room log huts with wind and rain blowing in through the cracks, and dirt floors soaking up moisture. We had no furniture, so we slept on rags and straw." As time went on, slave homes on some plantations improved. Slaves built themselves sturdier cabins, but most of them had no glass for windows and only a few pieces of homemade furniture.

But as hard as their lives were, slave families managed to make their own good times. They celebrated holidays in the

Slaves Invented Their Own Language

Africans from different tribes spoke different languages, and some slaves in the South couldn't understand one another. In time, they invented their own language, a mixture of African languages and English. Some people who live on the coast of South Carolina and Georgia still speak that language, known as Gullah.

slave quarters by giving each other homemade gifts, eating special foods, dancing, and singing. White people thought slaves sang because they were happy, but the opposite was true. Most of the songs that they sang told of Hebrew slavery in ancient times. The slaves felt that these songs also applied to them. Some slaves also sang African songs that had been handed down through generations.

Northern Slaves

Most slaves in the North lived very different lives from slaves in the South. Compared with large southern plantations, farms in the North were small. Male slaves on northern farms tended their owner's crops and animals, while most slave women worked in homes. Some slave owners in port cities hired out their slaves to work on coastal ships, in shipyards, and in rope and sail factories. The slave owners kept the slaves' wages for themselves.

A visitor to Boston in 1687 wrote that no home in Boston was without one or two slaves. The same was probably true in other northern cities. Some city

A slave greets his owner in a northern home.

17

slaves lived in drafty shacks near their owners' homes. Most slaves slept in back rooms, attics, or closets in the owner's house. Sojourner Truth, a slave in New York at the end of the 1700s, slept in a damp cellar on a hard board with a thin blanket and some straw. "Like a horse," she said.

Slaves Worked The Land

Many slaves worked on tobacco fields, like the one shown here.

In Virginia, slaves planted, tended, and harvested tobacco crops. Tobacco had become a popular crop for farmers in the 1600s. People in America and Europe had begun smoking, sniffing, or chewing tobacco, and planters there became rich.

Presidents' Slaves

John Adams of Massachusetts, and his son, John Quincy Adams, were the only two of the first several presidents of the United States who didn't own slaves.

Thomas Jefferson owned many slaves, including Sally Hemings. It has been said that he was the father of at least one of Hemings' children.

Some slave owners, or their drivers, whipped their slaves to make them work harder. Other owners rewarded hard work by giving their slaves free time to earn money for themselves. These slaves then sold baskets they had made, fish they had caught, or meat they had hunted to whites and free blacks. Isaac, one of George Washington's slaves, kept bees and sold the honey.

After a time, the planters were afraid slaves with money would become too independent, so it became illegal to buy things from slaves. Other laws also kept slaves dependent on their masters. For example, slave owners eventually decided that slaves wouldn't want to work in fields or homes if they could read and write, so it became illegal to teach them how.

In South Carolina and Georgia, another important crop flourished. The area's hot, humid climate and swampy land were good for growing rice. The colonial planters didn't know how to grow rice because England had been too cold for rice farming. Slaves who had grown rice in Africa showed them how.

The slaves had to make some changes because of the nature of the land. For example, rivers in these states flowed from the

Slaves load the rice crops onto boats.

ocean into the swamps, so the slaves built earthen dams to keep saltwater out of the swamps in which the rice was to be planted. Mosquitoes that spread a disease called malaria stung the slaves as they worked up to their knees in mud, clearing trees and undergrowth, planting seeds, and pulling out weeds. The slaves also dug reservoirs to hold fresh water and canals to take it to the crops. They harvested and **threshed** the rice, beating the grains from the husks. Then they bundled the rice, piled it onto barges, and took it down the rivers to the ocean, where it was shipped to England and sold.

By the end of the 1700s, rice and tobacco were not selling as well because these crops were now being grown in European countries and their colonies in Southeast Asia. Growing cotton was more popular because a new machine made harvesting cotton faster and easier. So to make extra money, some tobacco and rice planters sold off some slaves. Slave owners separated slaves from their families, chained the slaves together, and marched them hundreds of miles farther south. Those who survived the trip were sold at fairs, taverns, stores, at businesses dealing with animals and farm supplies, and in auctions.

War's End Brings Change

The colonists fought the Revolutionary War (1775–1783) to free themselves from Britain. At that time, the slaves thought about their freedom too. "If one minute's freedom had been offered to me, and I had been told I must die at the end of that minute, I would have taken it just to stand one minute on God's earth a free woman," Elizabeth Freeman said later.

In 1781, Elizabeth and her sister Lizzy worked as household slaves in the English colony of Massachusetts. Elizabeth's eyes widened as she entered the kitchen one morning. Their mistress held a red-hot fireplace shovel high in the air and she was about to strike Lizzy with it. Elizabeth ran across the kitchen and stepped between them. The shovel struck her arm

Elizabeth Freeman won her battle for freedom in court.

and cut her flesh down to the bone. Elizabeth carried the scar for the rest of her life.

While she was working in her owner's home, Elizabeth heard a visiting lawyer talk about freedom. She went to see him, and she asked if there was any way she could be freed. He took her case to court. He told the jury that although slavery had been legal in the past, Massachusetts' new constitution and the Declaration of Independence both stated that all people were born free and equal. The lawyer said that Elizabeth should be freed. The jury agreed. Two years later, slavery was **abolished**, made illegal, in Massachusetts. Elizabeth's case had led the way.

In 1783, the Revolutionary War ended, and Great Britain **ceded**, or surrendered, the southern Mississippi Valley to the United States. After the war, slavery became illegal in some northern states, but was still legal in southern states.

Fugitive slaves ride north to escape from slavery in the South.

Chapter Three

Runaways and Rebels

Thousands of slaves ran away—some alone, others with families or friends. Many joined communities of escaped African and American Indian slaves in forests, mountains, and swamps. Some slaves hid with free blacks in southern cities or stowed away on trains and boats that were headed north.

Many slaves escaped using the "Underground Railroad"—a secret system created by free blacks and whites to help slaves in the South escape to the

A Desperate Mother

Harriet Jacobs, a slave in North Carolina in the 1800s, looked down at her sleeping baby, and hoped her son would die. Death was better than slavery, she thought. Her son didn't die, but some slave mothers were so desperate they killed their children so that they wouldn't have to live in slavery.

Harriet escaped slavery after years of being mistreated by her owner. She ran away and hid in a tiny crawl space above her grandmother's shed. After months of searching, her master figured Harriet had gone north, and he sold her children to their father. Luckily, their father brought them to her grandmother's house.

North. A "station" might be a farm where runaway slaves hid in a hayloft, a house where they hid in a closet, or a store where they hid in an upstairs room. "Passengers" referred to escaped slaves, and "conductors" were people who helped the runaway slaves, or "passengers," on their way.

One famous conductor was Harriet Tubman. At the age of thirteen, Harriet tried to save another slave from being punished. An overseer threw a heavy weight at her and fractured her skull. Harriet escaped through the Underground Railroad three years later, and returned to the South nineteen times to lead more than three hundred slaves to freedom.

During one rescue mission, Harriet Tubman and the fugitives boarded a train headed south to avoid suspicion. On another mission, when her former master approached, she freed some live chickens she had bought, and turned around to chase them to avoid having him see her face.

Some slaves invented creative ways to escape. Ellen Craft's husband had dark skin; her skin was light. They decided to go north, so that their baby would be born in freedom. Ellen cut her hair, wore men's clothes, and wrapped her beardless face in a shawl. They traveled by boat and train as a slave owner with a toothache and his slave. Slave catchers pursued them to Boston, so **abolitionists**, people who worked to abolish slavery, sent the Crafts to England, where they lived in safety. Lear Green shipped herself to freedom in a sailor's chest. Henry

Harriet Tubman (on the far left) stands with some of the people she helped rescue from slavery in the South.

27

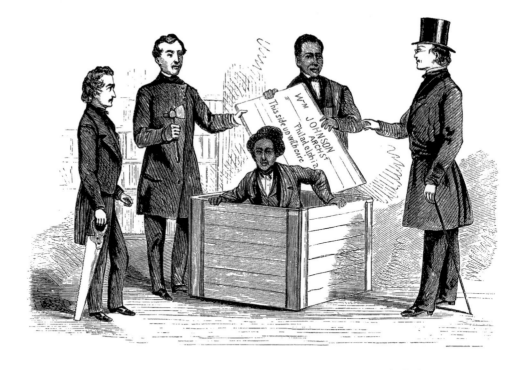

To escape slavery, Henry Brown mailed himself north in a packing crate.

Flogging for a Fee

For twenty-five cents, slave owners in Charleston, South Carolina, could have their slaves flogged at a special place called the Workhouse.

Brown went from Richmond, Virginia to Philadelphia, Pennsylvania in a packing box.

Slaves who tried to escape knew that they would be punished if they were caught. Slaves could receive a **flogging**, imprisonment, dismemberment, or branding with a red-hot iron for running away. When Moses Roper, an escaped slave, was caught, his hands were tied to a rope and a **pulley**, or a wheel. He was hauled up and down from the ceiling for hours as a horse attached to the other end of the rope moved around and around.

In 1850, Congress passed a law that made it easier to capture runaway slaves in northern states. Anyone who helped slaves could be jailed, fined, or both. In 1851, Shadrach, an escaped slave, was arrested and taken to the Boston court-

house. Some free blacks rushed in when guards left the room, marched Shadrach out, and helped him escape to Canada.

Abolitionists hung black material on their doors and windows and chanted "Freedom is Dead" as soldiers marched runaways Thomas Sims and Anthony Burns down Boston's Long Wharf and placed them on steamboats headed south.

The new law forced many slaves to escape further north. After the stricter Fugitive Slave Law was passed, Harriet Tubman took runaways all the way to Canada. She said that she no longer trusted Uncle Sam—the U.S. government—with her people.

Rebel Slaves

Despite the risks and the possible punishments, slaves resisted authority in many ways. Sometimes they worked slowly. Sometimes they burned down houses, stables, and haystacks. In 1739, slaves in Charleston, South Carolina, stole guns from a store and killed twenty people before English soldiers attacked the slaves' camp and killed fourteen of them. The rest were questioned and shot.

In 1799, a slave called Gabriel, a Virginia blacksmith who had once been branded with a hot iron for stealing a pig, secretly heated and hammered metal to make clubs and bayonets. He and about nine hundred other slaves on his master's plantation plotted to take over the city of Richmond. A sudden rainstorm flooded the roads, preventing them from reaching the city. Some returned to the plantation, but Gabriel and twenty-seven of his men were rounded up and hanged.

Denmark Vesey became a Methodist minister in Charleston, South Carolina, after he won a lottery and bought his freedom. In 1818, the city closed his church because so many slaves, free blacks, and some whites had joined the congregation that slave owners were afraid the church had become too powerful.

Vesey had a plan to free slaves and many people helped. A blacksmith made daggers and bayonets. A white barber made wigs and whiskers from European hair so light-skinned blacks could disguise themselves and enter Charleston without being stopped. Authorities learned of the plan, and rounded up hun-

Caught

Fierce dogs and armed slave catchers tracked down runaways and returned them to their owners. In the 1800s, slave owners paid slave catchers about $200 to bring back a runaway.

Authorities caught Nat Turner six weeks after the rebellion.

dreds of blacks—most of whom knew nothing about it. Vesey and thirty-four others were hanged. Whites who had helped them were fined and thrown into prison.

Nat Turner of Virginia believed that God wanted him to punish whites for enslaving blacks. At midnight on August 21, 1831, he and seven other slaves began to kill whites. They were joined by fifty or sixty other slaves, and the violence continued until at least fifty-seven whites lost their lives. Soldiers and sailors rounded up hundreds of African-Americans. Some of them knew nothing about the rebellion, but they were whipped and killed anyway. Nat Turner was hanged.

William Lloyd Garrison was a leading supporter of "the cause."

Chapter Four

The Cause

Abolitionists called working for slaves' freedom "the cause." They formed societies, held meetings, and published books, newspapers, sermons, and pamphlets to educate people on the evils of slavery. Many whites, even abolitionists, were racists—people who think one race is not as good as another. Some whites still believed blacks were better off in slavery, and had been created just to serve whites. Other people knew that slavery was wrong, but didn't want to give up their comfortable, profitable way of life. Some were afraid that freeing the slaves would cause trouble.

Abolitionists faced angry mobs and the possibility of injury or death for their beliefs. Slavery supporters attacked free blacks in the streets during antislavery conventions in Boston and Philadelphia, and one African-American man drowned as he tried to swim across a river to escape a mob. The homes and churches of African-Americans, and the hall where the Women's Anti-Slavery Convention was held, were set on fire. Stones were thrown at black and white women as they left the burning building arm in arm.

Boston merchants who did business with the South accused the abolitionists of being **agitators**. The merchants wrote angry letters to other newspapers when William Lloyd Garrison, publisher of *The Liberator*, an antislavery newspaper in Boston, wrote about the evils of slavery. The merchants said that he would ruin their trade with the South.

In his newspaper (shown below), William Lloyd Garrison wrote articles against slavery.

During the 1800s, Garrison was jailed in Baltimore for calling the owner of a slave ship a "robber," and pulled through Boston streets on a rope for writing that all men were equal.

THE LIBERATOR.

VOL. I.]   WILLIAM LLOYD GARRISON AND ISAAC KNAPP, PUBLISHERS.   [NO. 22.

BOSTON, MASSACHUSETTS.]   OUR COUNTRY IS THE WORLD—OUR COUNTRYMEN ARE MANKIND.   [SATURDAY, MAY 28, 1831.

People pelted Garrison with rotten eggs as he spoke at a meeting and struck him with stones as he left his office. "I will be heard," he wrote when he was threatened with hanging. He continued to work for the cause.

Many others wrote and spoke against slavery. Frederick Douglass, a fugitive slave, became a famous writer, newspaper publisher, and a great **orator** at abolitionist meetings. He broke his hand when he was attacked in a small Indiana town.

David Walker, the son of a slave father and a free mother, sewed antislavery pamphlets into the pockets of secondhand clothes he sold in Boston. The state of Georgia offered $10,000 to anyone who would deliver him to the state alive, or a $1,000 to anyone who killed him. In 1830, he was found dead near the doorway of his shop. William Still, the son of slaves, bought his own freedom and became secretary of the Pennsylvania Abolition Society. He kept careful records of the more than six

Frederick Douglass gave his first antislavery lecture in 1841.

hundred runaway slaves he had helped, so that their relatives and friends could find them.

Women Abolitionists

Some of the women who joined the abolitionist cause also spoke out for women's rights. Sojourner Truth, an escaped slave, said that when women got their rights they would not

Sojourner Truth fought for the abolition of slavery and for equal rights for all women.

have to ask men for money. She also said that slave owners owed slaves so much that if they paid it all back they would have no money left to buy seed for their crops. She said that all owners could do was **repent**—ask God for forgiveness—and the debt would be forgiven.

Women worked for the cause in several ways. In 1833, Prudence Crandall, a white teacher, was arrested for running a boarding school for free black girls in Connecticut. Abby Kelly, a Quaker teacher from Massachusetts, organized women to distribute pamphlets and speak in different parts of the country. Lucy Stone, who later became a leader in the women's **suffrage** movement,

Harriet Beecher Stowe's book, Uncle Tom's Cabin *(shown here), influenced a lot of people's opinions about slavery.*

was drenched with cold water as she spoke at an antislavery meeting. The Grimké sisters were born into a wealthy South Carolina slave-owning family. The sisters left the South and went north because they hated slavery, and became writers, speakers, and antislavery organizers. To raise money, women sold cakes and pies, and pens labeled "Abolitionist Weapons" at holiday fairs. Harriet Beecher Stowe, wrote *Uncle Tom's Cabin*, a book that influenced more people to join the cause.

The Missouri Compromise

Settlers' Nicknames

Missouri **proslavers,** people for slavery, who crossed into Kansas were called "border ruffians." Antislavery settlers were known as "free soilers."

By 1850, the United States stretched all the way to the Pacific Ocean. Arguments arose in Congress because Southerners wanted slavery in new territories and states. They were afraid slavery would be voted out of existence if there were more congressmen from free states than slave states. The Missouri Compromise seemed to solve the problem. Missouri was admitted as a slave state, and Maine came into the Union as a free state. The compromise also outlawed slavery in any new territories north of Missouri's southern border, except for Missouri itself.

The Kansas and Nebraska territories were both north of Missouri's southern border, so according to the Missouri Compromise, they should be free states, but southern congressmen wanted them to be slave states. Four years later another argument arose. Western congressmen wanted the **transcontinental,** or coast to coast, railroad to take a central route while Southern congressmen wanted the railroad closer to their states. Senator Stephen Douglas of Illinois suggested another compromise. The railroad would take the central route if people in Kansas and Nebraska could decide the slavery question for themselves. This compromise was called the Kansas-Nebraska Act.

At first, few people settled in Nebraska, but hundreds rushed into Kansas. Southern slave owners brought slaves to Missouri with them. The slave owners frequently crossed into Kansas and attacked antislavery settlers, most of whom were from New England, and tried to drive them out, because the slave owners wanted Kansas to have a majority of voters who would vote to allow slavery.

This illustration shows supporters of slavery crossing into Kansas.

Violence in the U.S. Senate

Senator Charles Sumner of Massachusetts spoke in the Senate the day Lawrence, Kansas, was attacked. He said that by helping to make Kansas a slave state, South Carolina's senator Andrew Butler had "taken slavery as his mistress." Two days later, Butler's nephew, Congressman Preston Brooks, entered the Senate chamber, lifted his gold-headed cane, and struck Sumner so hard that the cane broke into pieces. Senator Sumner didn't recover for three years. Charleston merchants bought Brooks a new cane engraved "Hit Him Again."

In 1855, proslavers won an illegal election in the territory of Kansas—six thousand votes were cast, but only three thousand voters lived there. Border ruffians made up the difference. In 1856, John Brown, an abolitionist from the east, and his followers helped thirty-five free soilers defend themselves against a hundred border ruffians in Osawatomie, Kansas, near the Missouri border. A short time later, hundreds of proslavery men captured free soilers in Lawrence, Kansas, burned buildings, and raised South Carolina's flag over the town's antislavery headquarters. In return, John Brown and his men raided a proslavery settlement on Pottawatomie Creek and killed five settlers. A number of other small battles broke out between border ruffians and free soilers, and another fifty people were killed. The conflict ended in 1859 after a legal election was held, and Kansas adopted an anti-slavery constitution.

One Man's War

In 1859, John Brown and twenty-two men, including five blacks, captured the U.S. **arsenal** in Harpers Ferry, Virginia (now West Virginia). Brown planned to use the weapons in the

John Brown

John Brown's family, like most abolitionists, believed slavery was against God's law, and the Browns helped many runaways escape to Canada. John saw slavery first-hand when he was twelve and spent a few days in a rich man's home. The man's slave, who was also about twelve, was ill fed, forced to sleep in the cold, and beaten with anything his owner had handy.

When he grew up, John Brown organized a group of blacks in Massachusetts to protect themselves from slave catchers. He and his family lived in North Elba, New York, where many escaped slaves lived. Blacks and whites there worked and played together and visited each other's homes. Some abolitionists thought freed slaves should be sent back to Africa, but John Brown disagreed. By that time, most slaves had been born here, and some of their families had been here for more than two hundred years.

This illustration shows U.S. forces capturing John Brown in Harpers Ferry, Virginia.

arsenal to establish a fort, from which to lead raids to free slaves throughout the South.

Colonel Robert E. Lee of the United States Army and some U.S. Marines recaptured the arsenal the next day. Brown was wounded in the fight, and ten of his men, including two of his sons, were killed. Brown was tried for **treason**, betraying one's country. He was found guilty and hanged. Proslavery people called him a **fanatic**—a mentally unbalanced person—but abolitionists called him a hero, though most did not agree with his violent methods. The day he was hanged, John Brown wrote: "I, John Brown, am now quite certain the crimes of this guilty land will never be **purged**, but with blood."

He was right. The Civil War was on its way.

Civil War

A civil war is a war fought within a country, rather than against another country.

43

Dred Scott took his legal battle for freedom all the way to the United States Supreme Court.

Chapter Five

The Civil War

When Dred Scott moved to Illinois with his master, slavery was illegal so Scott went to court to claim his freedom. His case went all the way to the Supreme Court, the highest court in the United States. In 1857, its chief justice said that no black person could claim U.S. citizenship, and Scott was still a slave. Abraham Lincoln was a lawyer in Illinois at that time. The Supreme Court decision was wrong, he said, when he ran against Stephen Douglas for his seat in the U.S. Senate. It meant slavery would continue to spread.

Lincoln–Douglas Debates

Abraham Lincoln and Stephen Douglas debated several times. Some historians have said that Lincoln was racist because, when he was trying to get elected, he said he did not intend to make blacks equal to whites. But he also said slavery was wrong, and that the Declaration of Independence said all men were created equal. In a letter to a friend, he wrote that seeing slaves chained together on steamboats made him feel miserable, and he hated to see the "poor creatures" hunted down.

Lincoln lost his bid for the Senate, but because of the debates, he became the country's leading antislavery politician, and in 1860 he was elected president. Slave owners were afraid he wouldn't let them keep their slaves, so South Carolina **seceded** from the Union, as the United States was often called. By the time Lincoln took office, six more Southern states had withdrawn, and four others were about to join them. Together they formed a new country, called the Confederate States of America, or the Confederacy. Lincoln could see its flag flying over buildings in Arlington, Virginia, from his office window.

A Nation Divided

When Lincoln took his oath of office on March 4, 1861, sharpshooters were stationed on nearby rooftops, detectives mingled with the crowd, and cannons stood on a nearby hill. The night before, detectives had learned of a plot to kill Lincoln and added extra security measures to protect him. In his speech, Lincoln said that a husband and wife could divorce and leave each other, but different parts of our country could not. "In your hands, my dissatisfied countrymen, . . . is the issue of civil war."

Only a month after Lincoln became president, tensions between the North and South increased over Fort Sumter. Fort Sumter was on an island in Charleston, South Carolina's harbor, and the Confederates demanded that the fort be turned over to them. Major Robert Anderson, of the U.S. Army, who was in charge of the fort, refused. Confederate cannons fired until the U.S. flag was lowered, and Major Anderson and his soldiers left. On April 15, President Lincoln called on his troops to take back the fort. The Confederates considered the president's call a declaration of war and the Civil War began.

Confederate troops fired cannons at Fort Sumter in April 1861.

The South was mainly agricultural. The North had weapons factories, railroads to move soldiers, and ships to **blockade** Southern ports. Most people thought the Union would soon win, and the war would end. Lincoln called for seventy-five thousand volunteers to enlist in the Union army for ninety days. Ninety days was not long enough. The Confederacy had more experienced military men than the Union had. Jefferson Davis, the Confederacy's president, had been a soldier and U.S. secretary of war. Lincoln had no military experience at all.

The first battle of the war took place on July 21, 1861, at Manassas, Virginia, 25 miles (40 kilometers) from Washington, D.C. News of the coming battle leaked out, and people who had never seen one went to watch the fighting. The Union army fell apart soon after the spectators spread their blankets on a nearby hillside. Soldiers and spectators fled back to Washington. The North continued to lose, so President Lincoln bought some books on military matters and stayed up late studying them. When he felt he knew enough about military **strategy**, he began to direct the war and the Union started to win.

On November 19, 1863, Lincoln gave a short speech at Gettysburg, Pennsylvania, where thousands of men on both sides had been killed. He said the war was being fought so that ". . . this nation, under God, shall have a new birth of freedom, and that government of the people, by the people, for the people shall not perish from the earth." That speech, called the Gettysburg Address, is carved on a plaque in the Lincoln Memorial in Washington, D.C.

Free At Last

At first, Lincoln thought the war's only goal was to bring the South back into the Union. Then he realized that even if the South returned to the Union, there would be no peace unless the slavery problem was settled. So, in 1863, while the war was still being fought, he freed all slaves in the Confederacy by issuing a document called the Emancipation Proclamation. Blacks could now serve in the Union army and navy. Several all-black regiments were formed. When the war ended, more than 180,000 blacks, most of them freed slaves, had volunteered. They manned military forts, and fought in front lines and on ships.

In 1865, the South surrendered, and the Thirteenth **Amendment** was added to the U. S. Constitution, abolishing

This painting depicts Lincoln after he gave his speech in Gettysburg, Pennsylvania on November 19, 1863.

This illustration shows an event in Washington, D.C., celebrating the abolition of slavery.

slavery in the entire United States. The war had lasted for four years. Southern towns, cities, businesses, homes, and plantations were destroyed, and more American lives were lost than in any war before or since.

Life was still hard for slaves after they were freed. Where could they go? What could they do? Laws had kept most of them from learning to read and write. But slaves had cleared the wilderness in the new United States. They had dug its canals and laid its railroad tracks. They had worked in the factories and on the plantations that were the foundation of the U.S. economy. They had fought in its wars.

Some freed slaves continued to work as **tenant farmers** on the same plantations they had worked on as slaves. Now they had to pay rent and buy food and clothing with their meager earnings. Other freed slaves worked as **sharecroppers** for a small share of the planter's crop.

To help the former slaves make the transition from slavery to freedom, the U.S. government established the Freedmen's Bureau in 1865. The bureau provided for basic needs, such as food, shelter, and medical care as well as financed and built hundreds of schools for African-American children. Despite great opposition, the bureau also tried to protect African-Americans' civil rights.

This photo shows sharecroppers' homes in Virginia after the end of the Civil War.

Timeline

1808	Slave trade in the United States declared illegal, but continues.
1839	Africans rebel on Spanish ship *Amistad*.
1850	Stricter Fugitive Slave Law is passed.
1856	Slave owners attack Lawrence, Kansas.
1857	Supreme Court decides Dred Scott is still a slave.
1859	John Brown raids Harpers Ferry.
1860	Abraham Lincoln is elected president of the United States.
1861–1865	Northern and Southern states battle each other in Civil War.
1863	Abraham Lincoln issues Emancipation Proclamation.
1865	Thirteenth Amendment to the U.S. Constitution abolishes slavery.

Glossary

abolished—did away with entirely

abolitionist—a person who wanted all slavery abolished

agitator—a troublemaker

amendment—a change in an existing law

arsenal—a storage place for weapons

barracoon—a jail or pen for slaves in Africa

blockade—surround, cut off

ceded—surrendered, released

fanatic—a person thought to be unbalanced or mentally ill

flogging—whipping

orator—a good speaker

pest house—a holding place for sick slaves

proslaver—a person in favor of slavery

plantation—an estate on which workers lived

pulley—a wheel around which rope is wound in order to lift and lower something

purged—cleansed

repent—to ask God to forgive for something one is sorry to have done

seceded—withdrew from

sharecropper—a freed slave who worked on owner's land and received part of the crop as payment

strategy—scientific planning

suffrage—the right to vote

tenant farmer—a person who farms other peoples' land and pays rent in money or a share of the crops

threshed—beat grains from husks

transcontinental—from coast to coast

treason—betraying one's country

To Find Out More

Books

Black, Wallace. *Slaves to Soldiers, African-American Fighting Men in the Civil War*, New York: Franklin Watts, 1998.

Cooper, Michael. *From Slave to Civil War Hero, Life and Times of Robert Smalls*. New York: Dutton, 1994.

Freedman, Russell. *Lincoln, A Photobiography*. New York: Clarion, 1987.

Greene, Jacqueline. *Slavery in Ancient Egypt and Mesopotamia*. Danbury, CT: Franklin Watts, 2000.

_____. *Slavery in Ancient Greece and Rome*. Danbury, CT: Franklin Watts, 2000.

Hamilton, Virginia. *Many Thousands Gone*. New York: Knopf, 1993.

Lyons, Mary. *Letters from a Slave Girl*. New York: Simon and Schuster, 1992.

Newman, Shirlee P. *The African Slave Trade*. Danbury, CT: Franklin Watts, 2000.

———. *Child Slavery in Modern Times*. Danbury, CT: Franklin Watts, 2000.

Videos

Africans in America: America's Journey Through Slavery. WGBH Boston Video, 1998.

Amistad. DreamWorks SKG and Home Box Office. Dream-Works Distribution L.L.C., 1997.

Beloved. Walt Disney Productions and Harpo Films. Distributed by Buena Vista Pictures, 1998.

Frederick Douglass: When the Lion Wrote History. PBS Home Video, 1994.

Glory. TriStar Pictures, 1989.

The Voyage of La Amistad—A Quest for Freedom. MPI Home Video, 1997.

Organizations and Online Sites

American Anti-Slavery Group
198 Tremont Street, #421
Boston, MA 02116
http://www.anti-slavery.org
This organization works to abolish slavery worldwide.

The DuSable Museum of African-American History
740 East 56th Place
Chicago, IL 60637-1495
http://www.dusablemuseum.org/
A museum devoted to African and African-American subjects.

The Charles H. Wright Museum of African American History
315 East Warren Avenue at Bush Street
Detroit, MI 48201
http://www.maah-detroit.org/
This museum presents exhibits on African and African-American history and culture.

The Museum of Afro American History
14 Beacon St., Suite 719
Boston, MA 02108
http://www.afroammuseum.org/
The museum presents exhibits, educational workshops, and special events devoted to the contributions of African-Americans during colonial times in New England.

A Note on Sources

Most of my research has been done using good, old reliable books. Internet sources on the slavery were not suitable, but adult books about slavery—some new, some old—were valuable, taken home from the library by the dozen, and compared. *Silent Terror, a Journey through Contemporary Slavery* was given to me by the president of the Anti-Slavery Society in Boston, Massachusetts. It is mostly about slavery today, but discusses the past too. I also consulted several encyclopedias. Milton Meltzer's books for children and young adults are great. I am indebted to him. I made special trips to Charleston, South Carolina; Savannah, Georgia; Newport, Rhode Island; and several islands in the West Indies for background material for this book. I also explored the replica of the 1700s ship *Bark Endeavor*. After I completed my research and wrote the first draft, Claude A. Clegg, III, University of Indiana at Bloomington, reviewed the manuscript and offered helpful suggestions. Thanks to Newton and Waltham Public Libraries, and Jeff, Jan, Paula, and Mark for trips to the Caribbean, South Carolina, and Georgia.

—*Shirlee P. Newman*

Index

Numbers in *italics* indicate illustrations.

About the Author

Shirlee Petkin Newman has written twenty books for children, including four for the Franklin Watts Indians of the Americas Series: *The Incas, The Inuits, The Creek*, and *The Pequots*, and three books in the Watts Library Slavery Series. Her books include biographies, a picture book, fiction, and folk tales. She has been an Associate Editor at *Child Life* Magazine and taught Writing for Children at Brandeis University. She has also written a historical fiction story set in Boston in Abolitionist times. She has traveled to North Africa, the Middle East, Europe, the Caribbean (West Indies), Central and South America, and Mexico.